HOW KIDS GROW

by JEAN MARZOLLO
Photographed by NANCY SHEEHAN

Cartwheel
·B·O·O·K·S·®

SCHOLASTIC INC.
New York   Toronto   London   Auckland   Sydney

For P-Quy
and her big sisters, Julia and Lucy,
who are watching her grow.
—J.M.

To my wonderful brother Michael, with love.
A special thanks to Icings Children's Boutique
for the beautiful clothes.
—N.K.S.

Go to www.scholastic.com for Web site information
on Scholastic authors and illustrators.

Text copyright © 1998 by Jean Marzollo.
Illustrations copyright © 1998 by Nancy Sheehan.
All rights reserved. Published by Scholastic Inc.
SCHOLASTIC, CARTWHEEL BOOKS and the CARTWHEEL BOOKS logo
are trademarks and/or registered trademarks of Scholastic Inc.

Library of Congress Cataloging-in-Publication Data
Marzollo, Jean
    How kids grow / by Jean Marzollo; photographed by Nancy Sheehan.
        p.   cm.
    Summary: Photographs show how children grow and change from tiny babies to six- and seven-year-olds.
    ISBN 0-590-45062-X
    1. Child development—Juvenile literature.   [1. Growth.   2. Child development.]   I. Sheehan, Nancy, ill.
II.Title.
    HQ767.9.M39 1998
    305.231—dc21   97-39190
                                                                                   CIP
                                                                                   AC

10 9 8 7 6 5 4 3   01 02

Printed in the U.S.A.   23
First printing, December 1998

Babies grow into kids.
As they grow, they change.
No two kids grow exactly
the same way at the same time.
But all kids grow,
and all kids are wonderful.
Each child is unique,
as you will see in these pictures.

James is three days old.
Even though he is a baby,
he can do many things.
Once he falls asleep,
he is a very good sleeper.

James can hold his
sister's fingers.

James likes to look at faces.
He likes to touch his
father's whiskers.

James loves to be cuddled.

Brittany is six months old.
She can lie on her tummy
and lift her head up.

Brittany's favorite toy is her rattle.
Shake it, shake it, Brittany!

She can roll over, too.

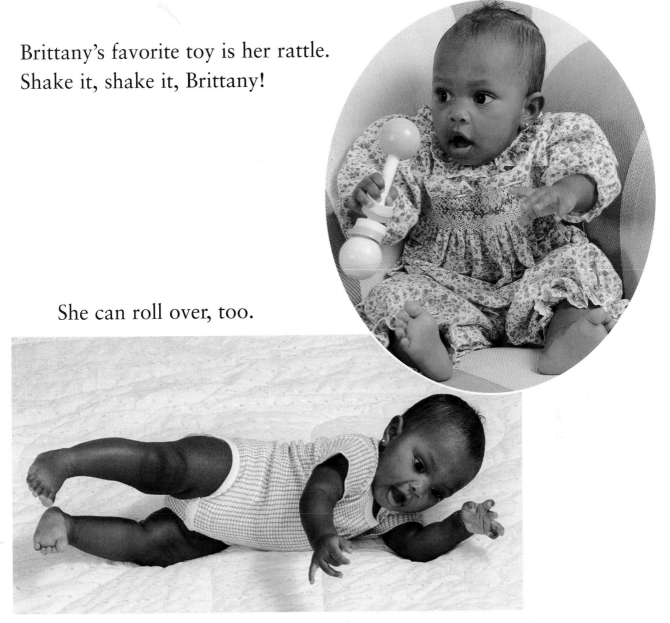

She needs to be in a safe place when she tries this skill.

Adeline is nine months old.
She likes to clap her hands.
Pat-a-cake, pat-a-cake,
Baker's man!

Adeline can feed herself
with her fingers.

Adeline is learning
how to crawl.
Hello, world.
Here I come!

Steven is one year old.
He is learning how to walk
all by himself.

He is learning how to talk, too.
Steven can say "Mama" and "Papa."
He calls the dog "Da."

Steven likes to wave bye-bye.
Bye-bye, Papa! Bye-bye!

Bobby is one and
a half years old.
He can scribble on paper.

Bobby has twelve teeth!
If you ask him to,
he can point to them.
He can point to his
nose and eyes, too.

Bobby's favorite toy
is a pretend lawnmower.
Vroom! Vroom!

Hanna is two.
She can drink from a cup.

If she holds on to the railing,
Hanna can walk up stairs.

Hanna likes to look
at the pictures in books.
She likes to listen to
the words.
She also likes to help
turn the pages.

Mark is two and a half.
He doesn't need diapers anymore.
He uses the potty.
Thumbs up, Mark!

Mark can talk in sentences.
For example, he can ask
his teddy bear,
"Do you want a kiss?"

Mark can build a tower of blocks,
knock it down,
and build it up again.

Noël is three years old.
She can ride a tricycle.

She can walk up *and down* stairs.
Don't forget to hold on, Noël!

Noël can put
a puzzle together.

Alex is three and a half years old.
He can jump off the ground
with both feet!

Alex can say his whole name.
"I am Alex Shaievitz!"

Alex likes to string
big wooden beads.

Olivia is four.
She likes to pretend she's a monster.
Roar-r-r-r!
Does she scare you?

Olivia can help clean up.

She can put on her pajamas.

Welby is five.
He can help make chocolate pudding.

He can write his name.

He can catch a ball, too!

Annie is six.
She can write a story.

Annie can
follow rules.
She likes to
play games.

She has just learned to ride a bicycle.

Adrienne is seven.
She has a loose tooth.

Adrienne can count from 1 to 50.
She can write from 1 to 10.

Adrienne can do
a cartwheel!
Whee!

 # I AM ME! I AM SPECIAL!

My name is _____.

I was born on _____.

I am now _____ years old.

Here's how I looked
when I was born.
(Paste or draw a picture
here of yourself as a baby.)

Here's how I look now.
(Paste or draw a picture
here of yourself today.)